An A of Worklife for Organisations

I'm Glad I Spent More Time at Work!

written by
Lynne H Copp

I'm Glad I Spent More Time At Work

An A to Z of Worklife Balance for Organisations

First Edition
First Published in England 2009

The right of Lynne H Copp to be identified as the Author of the work has been asserted by her in accordance with the Copyright, Designs and Patents Act 1998

All rights reserved. No part of this publication may be reproduced, stored in a retrieval system, or transmitted, in any form or by any means, electronic, mechanical, photocopying, recording or otherwise, without prior permission of Lollypop Publishing Ltd.

British Library Cataloguing in Publication Data
A catalogue record for this book is available from the British Library.

It is the policy of Lollypop Publishing Ltd. to use products that are recyclable and renewable made from wood from sustainable sources. The logging and manufacturing processes are expected to conform to the environmental regulations of the country of origin. We endeavour to minimise, where ever possible, the number of miles our products are transported.

Please share or recycle this book

Published by Lollypop Publishing Ltd.

Registered Office; Unit 1, Coombs Wood Court, Steel Park Road, Halesowen, B62 8BF

www.lollypoppublishing.co.uk

ISBN Number 978-1-906788-00-1

An A to Z of Worklife Balance for Organisations

I'm Glad I Spent More Time at Work!

SURREY LIBRARIES	
Askews	30-Oct-2009
658.314 ECO	£7.99

Lynne H Copp

Published by Lollypop Publishing Ltd.

I dedicate this book to
my darling daughters Cat & Jeni
and to my husband Kevin,
whose support, commitment, love and nagging
allow me to achieve balance too.

With special thanks to Kevin for his continued support and the free reign to go where my heart and passions take me. To my dear friend Beverley for her continued support and encouragement to do my writing and take my ideas and wisdom to a wider audience. To Sarah Marshall, my Publisher, for her patience, tenacity and graciousness. She has allowed me the space to write and the space to build my confidence too; allowing me to come forward when the time was right for me. To my co-coach and friend Ali Dawson; she has inspired my vision for what is possible and is a great coach and friend. To my mentors, coaches and advisors they are many, but especially to my English teachers at school; Mr Fenwick and Mr Cunningham who ignited the flames of my dream to one day be an author and publish many books. Finally, to all my clients and work associates who have provided me with a platform from which to learn, as well as to contribute;

I am sincerely grateful.

No one ever laid on their deathbed

wishing they'd spent more time at work!

Introduction

It is no longer appropriate to run organisations based on management practices that served us well in previous decades. The world of work, and the world of life, has changed too much for them to be appropriate today; or indeed tomorrow. Out of date 'command and control' leadership style merely guarantees the flood of attrition, negativity and mediocre bottom lines. In the metaphorical wardrobe of leadership practices, these styles are still worn by some, but no longer fit. It is time to de-clutter all the old and well-frayed leadership approaches and clear space for new and exciting styles that will take your business and people forward. Technology development, customer demands, employee demographics and the cost of doing business, means that the workplace, and its people, must be managed and led differently.

Employees come to work to do a good job and if given the right environment, will give their best. That environment must be built on trust, dignity, respect and choice. When working cultures provide no choice but the demands of presenteeism and long hours, imbalance and demotivation are the result. This in turn creates stress, absence, turnover of staff, reduced productivity and stunted business results.

For great employers, real balance comes from the knowledge that they have developed an organisation worth working for and staying with. The business results speak for themselves and employee satisfaction, motivation and retention is high. They attract and retain the best talent; whatever their age, gender or cultural background. The buzz of working for that organisation is evident in their profits, costs, people and customer loyalty.

It is time to structure our organisations and our people systems differently otherwise we run the risk of killing our businesses. It is the trusting and the visionary who have taken the first brave steps towards a new horizon. These organisations understand that to survive, they must change; and change quickly. Most of the rest may well catch up, but some will die because they held onto their outdated and short term ways of working:
RIP! ...What will your choice be?

Worklife Balance is not some 'touchy-feely-nice-to-have-for-parents' idea; this is bottom line business sense for everyone! Our society, our businesses, our families, friends, workmates, bosses and communities need us all to be able to contribute to every aspect of work and life; not just a one-dimensional, work-focused existence.

I was recently told that one employer had excluded a manager from their workplace for six months; not because of poor performance, but because he had worked 18 hours a day, 7 days a week for 3 years. Whilst I will not comment on why it took so long, I will say I am glad they did.

However, what I am not sure about is whether he will seek support for workplace addiction during his six month forced sabbatical. I call it addiction on purpose, because it is.

Just like alcohol, people or drugs, we can become addicted to work. However, 'work' is the only addiction that is rewarded. I continually see people promoted for perceived 'commitment'; measured in hours instead of contribution. In other words 'input' instead of 'output'.

What kind of society are we evolving when almost 50% of parents see their children for less than 2 hours a day? Or that up to 37% of men die in the first five years after retirement? Or that women are passed over for promotion in the 10 years after having a child?

Employees of all ages and backgrounds are demanding change; questioning the continuous grind and thankless work environments in which they are expected to perform from dawn until midnight!

I challenge you now to make your workplace different if you want to attract and keep the best.

What is Worklife Balance and Why is it Important?

When there is balance between both sides of the scales in the diagram, then there is equilibrium; both sides are held in perfect balance by the pivot and arms that are joined to the base. If we consider the scales as

representations of our own worklife balance, then the pivot becomes our ability to balance the dishes on both sides that can become filled up with either work or life activities. Balance between both sides creates harmony and provides a sense of wellbeing. When the load is increased on either side, the scales tip towards work or towards life. When too much load is placed on both, the scales become stressed and can eventually snap. The same can happen in real life as well; too many demands from work and life can cause stress and if not addressed,

The A to Z of Worklife Balance

can eventually lead to a breakdown in wellbeing. It is natural for the scales to tip from side to side as long as they are able to return to their natural balanced position. In the same way, it is important that we recognise that our scales can tip towards work or life demands, but don't tip one way permanently; all play and no work, or all work and no play are just as detrimental to health and wellbeing.

What is Work?

Work is a source of income, a vocation or career, a sense of purpose and a social environment. Work that has meaning, plays to an employee's strengths and provides development is best for balance. An environment that releases potential, creativity and delegates ownership, is good for productivity and motivation.

People who love what they do and do what they love are generally more productive, loyal and efficient. Cultures that create this, in an environment where people are not imprisoned by long hours, poor leadership and short-termism, reap the benefits of productivity in a realistic and balanced way.

When the scales need to tip towards work due to impending deadlines workload or customer need, employees are usually willing to work

longer and harder to get the job done. In this organisation, they know that when the pressure is off, the scales will tip back to equilibrium.

There is not an expectation that they will work long hours as a way of life: selling their very soul to work. Employees are TRUSTED to come to work to do a good job and RESPECTED for the work they do and the life they have outside. This is a culture that creates DIGNITY at work where there is give and take for both the organisation and the employee.

Work is important; it pays the bills, provides a sense of purpose and engages our talents. However, when the scales are always tipped towards work, there is little time for life, for relationships, for fun and that leads to an environment where employees believe that they have NO CHOICE but to work. Equilibrium must be the goal, and it is the responsibility of the organisation and each employee to create it.

What is Life?

Life includes family, friends, leisure, learning and time for self; all the things that we work for. When work and life are not in balance, the result is stress, guilt, sacrifice and regret. Employees often report that they feel caught in a tug of war "I feel guilty if I go home on time and I feel guilty if I don't go home on time!"

To create balance between the two dishes named 'work and life', we must look at the pivot (the tipping point between work and life) and the base of the scales (the foundation on which everything sits). The pivot is owned by the employee and provides the indicator of balance (which is often unique to each person). Whereas the base is owned by the employer, as it is they who provide a solidfoundation that allows the employee to create their own equilibrium.

When implementing a worklife strategy into your organisation, keep it simple and straightforward - KISS. A kiss is often depicted using the letter X. In the diagram across we use the letter X to illustrate our simple approach to developing a worklife strategy

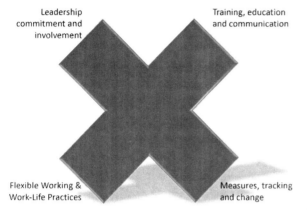

1. Leadership commitment and involvement

2. Training, education and communication

3. Flexible working and other work practices

4. Measures, tracking and change

In addition to the four elements of the strategy, there are also five indicators or measures of change, these are highlighted in the five circles below and are:

Culture - building trust and respect

Leadership - building inspiration, direction and involvement

Management - building consistency, openness and support

Employee Environment - respecting diversity, delivering dignity, empowerment, motivation and recognition

Infrastructure - Systems built to set people free, encourage innovation and challenge the status quo

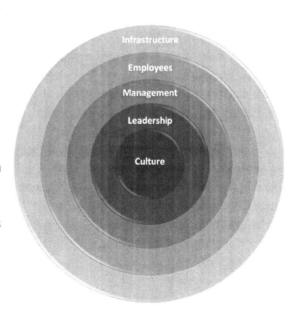

I'm Glad I Spent More Time at Work!

Worklife balance is therefore about creating dignity at work. When we respect people's need for balance, we respect difference and this delivers fantastic business results. People come to work to give their best, not to be judged for their colour, gender, sexuality, physical ability, mental capability, religion, beliefs, height, weight or any other aspect of them or their life style. Creating an environment of balance supports diversity and a culture of inclusion. This makes a world of difference to your business results, culture and employee motivation.

If we demand long-hours and give no respect to people's lives, they will become demotivated, deliver substandard results and eventually leave. However, if we respect that life comes first and we create a culture of 'give and take', we will motivate employees to be loyal as well as productive. For example, a man died recently because of workplace stress and pressure caused by the relentless demands of his employer to be at work on a certain day. All he had asked was to go home early in order to attend his son's birthday party.

I cannot think of one sales target, one meeting or indeed, one phone call that could not have waited for two hours whilst a child's party took place. What kind of society are we breeding when the job of being a parent is less important than a sales target?

Economies lose billions of dollars each year due to sickness;, 46% due to worklife imbalance. Calculate 46% of your absence bill and then decide to manage attendance instead of punishing absence and measuring hours of work.

Finally, flexible working is a solution which neutralises the clock-watchers, rinses away the work-addicts and flushes out the shirkers! There are many options for flexibility and most are documented in this book. It is time to regard the clock differently and stop the 9 to 5 daylight hours tradition, set in place by farmers over 100 years ago! Time and task can be carved differently to gain maximum benefit for the business, for its customers and for its employees.

The clock is ticking... what are you waiting for?

It is up to you how you read the rest of this book, there is no right or wrong approach.

You can read it cover to cover in one sitting, then give it away to someone who needs it more.

You can read a page a day and make notes about what you will do differently in your organisation.

Or, you can dip in and out to suit your needs; a kind of paper coach when required.

A is for Absence, Attendance and Ask ..1
B is for Business Case, Boundaries and Busy ..3
C is for Change, Choice and Contribution ..5
D is for Dedicate, Diagnose and Differentiate ..7
E is for Equality, Employee and E-Support ..9
F is for Flexible, Fathers and Faith ..11
G is for Give & Take, Gift and Goals ..13
H is for Human, Honesty and Help ..15
I is for Individual, Irrelevant and Involvement ..17
J is for Judgement, Journey and Joy ..19
K is for Knowledge, Knowing and Keen ..21
L is for Leadership, Learning and Lesson ..23
M is for Motivation, Mother and Me-time ..25
N is for New, 'No!' and Need ..27
O is for Opportunity, Ownership and One ..29
P is for Policy, Pilot and Presenteeism ..31
Q is for Questioning, Quaint and Quantify ..33
R is for Responsibility, Reasons and Recognition ..35
S is for Self, Strengths and Stress ..37
T is for Time, Talent and Transition ..39
U is for Universal, Understanding and Unleash ..41
V is for Virtual, Visionary and Victory ..43
W is for Wellbeing, Women and Workload ..45
X is for eXciting, X-Shaped and Xenophobic ..47
Y is for 'Yes!', Young and Year ..49
Z is for Zeal, Zest and Zenith...and Zzzz! ..51

A to Z

Is for Absence, Attendance and Ask

Most worklife imbalance related absence is due to employees taking sick leave to care for others; a sick child, dependant or friend. If an employee feels that it is easier to call in sick than ask permission to take time out for someone more important, they will. LIFE COMES FIRST. However, if you are able to create an environment where employees are empowered to take paid time off for emergencies, reduced absence, increased productivity and loyalty are the result.

Not feeling able to ask for emergency leave leads to stress, demotivation lack of productivity, increased sickness absence and attrition.

Focus on 'managing attendance' instead of 'managing absence'. The positive approach allows for creative methods to keep people in work, like:

• Incentivised attendance schemes

• Wellness programmes

• WARM interviews on return: **W**elcome back, **A**ssess fit for work, **R**esponsibility of manager and employee and **M**ove on!

- Involvement of managers

- Address any potential low morale or issues in departments

- Strengths based work design

- Flexible working – rearranged or reduced

Ask employees for their ideas on how to improve attendance, e.g. run focus groups to flush out the main reasons for absence and attrition, and then involve people in the solution.

Some employees take sick leave on days that they are expected to do their least preferred task, so set up a 'Job for a day' scheme - Find out what job they hate doing the most and you do it for a day! That way you can both look for ways to improve it. Remember, if you adopt strength-based work design, there are less 'least preferred' tasks to do!

Create a culture where it is 'OK' to ASK for time out if required. If an employee feels as though they can ask for a couple of hours to go to the garage to sort their car, you will get back increased productivity, reduced absence, reduced cost and reduced turnover of staff.

Ask for ideas on how to improve the working environment; both physical and emotional. This could be the catalyst for improvement schemes and employee led networks.

Finally, ask for the support of experts.

Don't try to do it all yourself.

Is for Business Case, Boundaries and Busy

Defining the business case for worklife balance and flexible working is key to getting started. To quantify the business case, begin to measure the general indicators and the cost implications. These general indicators are:

- Absence,

- Turnover of staff,

- Stress and pressure

- Workload and overwork

- Long hours

- Productivity

- Reduced employee and customer satisfaction.

It is also important to understand these issues by cutting the data in a way that identifies if there are any specific 'hotbeds' of imbalance, e.g. a certain department may have high absence. By measuring imbalance in this way, you will gain clarity and be able to prioritise your initiatives. After all there is no point in fixing what is not broken!

Boundaries are sometimes difficult things to put in place when you manage a team of remote workers or tele-workers. Managers still reject this mode of working because they cannot see and therefore cannot control the work done. In most cases, data shows that in fact, the home worker tends to work longer hours than their office based colleague. Therefore, effective boundary management means encouraging a clear delineation between work and life so that they are not always available or online. One client agrees 5 blocks of 1 hour when an employee will be 'unplugged' during a contracted working week. The manager doesn't care when the unplugged time is booked, but makes sure that it is reflected in his/her daily diary. That hour can be for lunch, or an early morning walk or an afternoon nap! It can be used for personal development, picking up children from school or playing sport. When unplugged, mobile phones, e-mail and other methods of contact are switched off. He has measured a 32% increase in productivity by introducing unplugged time for his sales team. He has also observed an increase in creativity and commitment. Supporting clear boundaries is an effective way of managing work and life. If you manage remote workers, make sure that you support them to create 'on' and 'off' time during their day, otherwise the boundaries between work and home become very foggy; which leads to a reduction in their effectiveness and increase in hours.

Being busy all the time does not mean being effective or productive. The brain works best in shorter bite-sized chunks of work with breaks in between. Busy periods should also be recognised and rewarded with timeout on less frenetic work or work that is focused on something completely different.

Is for Change, Choice and Contribution

The rate of change is accelerating and that impacts on the way organisations need to operate. Today's employees and customers have choice and will move to an organisation that provides them with the environment that they want. Changing to a flexible organisation that supports worklife balance means creating a culture that is embedded in trust and therefore provides CHOICE:

- Choice to work long hours to meet a deadline, but choice to take time off when the deadline is met

- Choice to support a sick relative and work from home whilst they are ill

- Choice to work reduced hours when a child is young Choice to flex hours to suit a customer need

- Choice to work a compressed working year to meet the demands of study time

Managing choice and change means recognising and understanding the human factors and building a culture that can be flexible enough to adapt to changing times. Remember, 98% of change projects fail because not enough attention is paid to the people aspects. Therefore, when you change your culture to one of flexibility, be sure to communicate choice and contribution at every opportunity.

Contribution is about what that person brings to the organisation; their strengths, competencies, skills, experience and knowledge. After all, that's why you hired them! Therefore, why not measure them on these things and stop measuring them on the time they spend in the office? Contribution can then be measured in terms of output, rather than input. In other words, Don't tell me how many hours you've worked; tell me what you have contributed towards our success!

Work with employees to explore what would work for their and the organisation's needs and allow them the ability to judge the flexibility they need at any given time.

Is for Dedicate, Diagnose and Differentiate

Rome wasn't built in a day and neither was the implementation of a new culture of flexibility and balance. Therefore, to facilitate success, it is good practice create a team of people from within the business who are dedicated to developing, implementing and reviewing worklife balance initiatives. The team should be made up of representatives from senior management, line management and employees. More information about the structure of this team can be found under 'Letter O'.

Whilst HR often champion worklife initiatives, it works better if they support the team and the organisation by acting as a trusted advisor and consultant instead of the owner of all initiatives. That way, the leadership and employees own it, and the burden is removed from the shoulders of HR.

The team's first job is the diagnosis of the current situation; to establish where it is starting from. The objective of this diagnosis or research is to understand where in the organisation imbalance is present, and what the main opportunities for change are. A proven method is to engage in a Worklife Evolution Review® which identifies where an organisation is on its journey towards a culture of excellence. The review measures all aspects of culture, leadership, management and employee environments. It makes recommendations, and supports the development of a vision towards becoming an employer of choice. Further details can be found at the back of this book. Once diagnosis is complete and a vision and strategy is in place, the team can then work on a blueprint for success and prioritise implementation based on the data that they have collected. Implementation is about action, owners, pilot projects, tracking and improving. It is essential that the team monitor progress and be clear about what is working and why.

The final part of this team's role is to differentiate the organisation through creative methods of communication, recognition and external assessment. This means linking all changes to performance and reward systems. It also includes comparison with other organisations through national and international awards and measurement systems. Finding ways to differentiate your organisation from any other means developing very different approaches. One client is currently focused on the psychology of colour and understanding how the five senses play a part in productivity and worklife balance. Differentiate through pioneering approaches.

Is for Equality, Employee and E-Support

Not everyone will want the same type of flexible arrangements and indeed, not everyone can be offered the same terms. As a manager, it is your responsibility to apply the rules and the decisions fairly and not be seen to be favouring any individual, team, or flexible option. Equality does not mean giving everyone the same, but it does mean considering each request with equal regard. For example, an employee may find it difficult to get to work for 6am because a recent illness has resulted in them losing their driving license. As their manager, you may support them to either start later or provide alternative transport. When another employee demands the same alternative transport, then unless they are incapacitated in the same way, the answer is 'no'. You have provided equal regard to the request, but the criteria for each case differs. Be open to reasons, and look for compromise where possible, but remember, if the business cannot support it, then it is OK to say 'no'. Look at N to find out more.

Worklife balance and flexible working is more successful if decisions about flexible working are owned at the employee level. When employees are involved in making decisions about their own flexibility, then they rarely take advantage. This is empowerment and it is not something you can delegate, but you can create it by letting go and allowing your team to take risks on new working patterns. By experimenting with different patterns, the team will find one that works for them and their customer. For example, one small design team of 10, worked 8 different flexible working practices. The team were so much more productive and creative as a result. They removed the stress of trying to work in a rigid way, thereby freeing them up to do a great job.

It may also be a good idea to communicate the options for flexible working and worklife balance on your intranet site. Call it 'e-flex' or 'e-balance'. Use the site to communicate best practice, provide access to request forms and links to other support, like policy information. One client uses the power of social networking to encourage worklife balance. She has created an internal social network where employees can engage support from each other.

Is for Flexible, Fathers and Faith

Flexible working makes business sense from a customer, as well as an employee perspective. Flexible working covers a wide range of options from part time to annualised hours. A guide to the most popular is contained at the back of the book and more information can be downloaded from our website. Flexibility can be considered for short-term as well as long-term needs. Remember, about 70% of your people will want to retain the pattern that they work already; not everyone needs or wants to change! That means that you are managing exceptions not opening floodgates!

Providing flexibility is the most effective method of attracting and retaining diversity of staff. For example, people over the age of 50 often want to reduce hours to take up other life pursuits, and parents sometimes need to look after school age children during holidays. Why not combine the two generations to create a job share over a year? The older person can cover the school holidays when the father is at home with the children, and the father can cover term time. This is a win-win for everyone: the organisation gets the job done and the employees meet their work and life needs.

If flexible working is new to your organisation, then why not focus on one area to pilot new ways of working? Focussing on one area allows you to test and measure the impact before rolling it out. For example, a 'Focus on Fathers' initiative can explore what kinds of flexibility work for dads in the organisation and why some men may feel reticent to try part time working or apply for parental leave. Alternatively, you may wish to focus on a specific group, like parents, carers, generations, ethnic backgrounds or faiths. Each area of focus is legitimate, but make sure that you always retain a vision of flexibility for all.

Faith-friendly workplaces are increasing as our employee populations become more diverse. Many organisations respect the employee's need to honour their particular faith or belief. For example, quiet rooms are set aside for prayer, or separate eating and storage areas for vegetarian food and of course flexible working to respect rituals and festivals. The benefits of creating a faith-friendly environment means that employers are now able to attract and retain a more diverse workforce, are able to create a more inclusive environment and are able to remove the need for rigid holiday periods that no longer serve the business or the customer.

Is for Give & Take, Gift and Goals

Worklife Balance is about the balance between work and life; not all work and not all life! Employees that are supported with life issues when they occur are more likely to be loyal, committed and productive than those who are unsupported. In fact, employees that operate in a supportive work environment are 26% more productive than their colleagues who are less cared for. In this sense, 'giving' really is 'receiving'. Equally, the business has needs too and it is sometimes important for employees to work longer hours to support a client deadline, or take on extra workload to support a department that is temporarily short of resource. This all means creating an environment of 'give and take'.

Giving to the organisation when required and taking back time as appropriate, or giving to life needs when required and taking back time for the organisation where appropriate. It is only when the scales are constantly tipped one way or the other, that imbalance and resentment occurs. For example, one employer asked a female worker to support a critical workplace project that would add to her existing workload. Both knew that it would mean long hours and focused commitment. The woman also knew that it would have a big impact on family life. The company said "Jill, if you do this project in the timescales required, we will reward you with a £5000 bonus." Jill saw that this was generous, but said, "If I do this, you can keep your £5000, but instead give me 7 weeks holiday with my children in the summer." They agreed; Jill did the work very successfully and spent the summer with her children. When she came back, she was more committed and loyal. Jill is still one of their top performers. Remember, the gift of time is often more appreciated than the gift of money for some employees.

Goals for worklife balance are essential and many organisations view "becoming an employer of choice" as their goal; but what will that look like? How will people be working, behaving, rewarded? Imagine that it is five years from now, create an image of your company, draw it, feel it, imagine it as if you have already achieved it. Involve as many people as you can in creating a part of the image. Then have a local artist paint it for you and put it in reception for everyone to see and strive to create.

Is for Human,
Honesty and Help

Many workplaces focus on getting the job done and forget to engage with the human doing the job. We are all human, and sometimes we have 'off' days or days when we are excited about something happening in our life. What can you do to increase the human aspects of work? Why not make sure that you know all employees' birthdays? Celebrate by sending them a card. Create ways you can celebrate their life priorities too; send a good luck e-mail when their child starts school, finishes their exams, passes their driving test or wins at rugby. These things help to engender teamwork, recognition, productivity and morale. Saying 'thank you' or 'well done!' once in a while supports people to feel appreciated for the work they do. For example, try a payslip message; each month at pay-day, send a note with the employee's payslip that is personalised and praises their contribution during the month. If delivered authentically, you will increase commitment, support and loyalty.

Honesty is one of the most important values that you should encourage in your team. It creates a culture of authenticity. A culture of authenticity prevents sickness absence for worklife issues, allows business needs to be communicated openly, builds trust and support in the team, prevents people taking advantage and reduces unhealthy conflict.

Providing help for employees when they need it most is essential; for their wellbeing and your business success. For example, if an employee is worried about a dying relative, they are unlikely to be focused on work. Taking time to ask what you can do to support them prevents costly and unsupportive situations developing. Avoiding the situation can be disastrous for both the business and individual. For example, one employee who was ignored and then punished for her lack of productivity during the time her mother was dying, simply left. The company lost a key worker and the employee lost their job as well as their mum. It costs at least £15,000 to replace a good employee; it may have cost less to give her the gift of time to be with her family.

Providing help that also protects the confidentiality of the employee and their family is also important. Good Employee Assistance Programmes, Wellbeing Centres or access to other support organisations via your intranet site, provides the ability to deal with sensitive situations without having to talk about it to colleagues.

Is for Individual, Irrelevant and Involvement

Treat people as individuals; they are as unique and individual as their handwriting! Get to know the individuality that each person brings and treat each worklife request as unique. No two people are the same and no person copes with a life or work issue in the same way. What may be trivial to you may be major to an employee. It is dangerous to assume; you could get it completely wrong. For example, two employees ask for flexible working: one is a parent of children and would like to start at 9:15 so he can drop his children to school; the second employee wants to start at 9:15 because she needed to muck-out and feed her horse. Based on your empathy with their life, and your judgements based on their contribution or work performance, you may be more sympathetic to one than the other. Worklife balance works best when a manager can view each request in a reason-neutral way. In other words, the reason that they request flexible working is irrelevant; the real question is whether the business can accommodate both of these employees arriving at 9:15. If one of them is the key-holder, then the business case suggests not. A compromise may have to be sought, e.g. finding another key-holder or flex their hours on a rota basis.

Don't try to come up with all the solutions yourself! Involvement of staff in new ways of working makes the change easier and they are more likely to be committed to it! For example, changing a shift pattern that has been in place for many years could be daunting for a manager in case it incites conflict with employees or unions. By involving all staff in the design, piloting and rollout, you are more likely to get buy-in and support because they will feel as though they own it.

One team who worked in a kitchen of a busy hotel knew that covering shifts was essential and absence or requests for time out at short notice were difficult to resource. The team purchased a big whiteboard calendar and everyone filled in planned dates like anniversaries, birthdays, children's sports days etc. Once all the important life dates were noted for the year, they could then manage the roster of cover and shift patterns. Absence reduced by 84%, because employees didn't take advantage of each other or of the business. Had they taken sick leave, it could have meant letting down and maybe even preventing a colleague from attending an important life event.

Is for Judgement, Journey and Joy

Never judge others based on your own frame of reference; you could get it wrong. Always try to maintain a position of complete neutrality. In counselling terms, it is referred to as 'maintaining a state of ignorance' in other words; ignore your own feelings and judgements, because they are yours, not your employees'. For example, if someone calls in to work and says, 'I can't come to work today because my cat is ill.' You may not empathise with this employee; especially if you hate cats! The cat might be the only thing that person has and therefore, its status is much higher than it would be in your life. To solve this issue, delegate the judgement to your employee. For example, ask the employee to put together a case for working flexibly. Encourage them to communicate it and get buy-in from their colleagues. Then work out a trial programme to test the new working practice (if it is to last longer than 3 months). If it goes well, formalise it, if not, improve it with your employee.

Worklife balance is a journey that is often easy and sometimes fraught with tough terrain. That means that it is important to implement worklife balance initiatives and strategies that project you towards a clear vision. There are many systems that can support you to measure where you are on your journey. Some of these are internal, some external like Worklife Evolution®. Take time to understand where you are headed and define the key milestones. At the start of the journey, make sure that you achieve some quick wins by implementing proven techniques, having the right team to support you and being equipped with up-to-date business knowledge so that you can project the future. Use a balanced scorecard to measure progress and achievements.

Joy is achieving the badge 'employer of choice'. It means that imbalance has been eliminated and employees find joy and meaning in the work that they do. They truly jump out of bed in the morning affirming "my company deserves me today!" Joy means self-fulfilment due to choice and support; it also comes from the joy of supporting others to be all they can be.

If joy and hope come from empowerment, then empowerment comes from taking risks and challenging the status quo. As one manager said "if you haven't taken a big risk in the past year, your life is too safe!" What risks will you take that create empowerment and energy in your teams? One client runs a 'dream' initiative, where employees have the chance to dream up new ways of working, or new ideas that will enhance the workplace.

Is for Knowledge, Knowing and Keen

Knowledge of your customer needs, your business needs and your employee needs, is a great starting point for developing a worklife strategy. For example, if you know that your customers are global, then operating a 9 to 5 environment may not make business sense as you will certainly need people to operate in different time zones. One company lost a major USA client because they would not change from their rigid 8 until 4 GMT working day.

Customers buy from people; especially people who look like, and behave like, them. Does your employee population reflect your customers' diversity? Diversity knowledge is also becoming more critical in the design of work. For example, Do you know what the different generations want from work? Or gender, ethnicity, race and sexual orientation? Understanding difference is an innovative way to look at flexibility, customer services and worklife practices.

- Know your customers inside out; know what they will need in the future as well as now and redesign your workplace to suit

- Know your business, the services and products you supply today and the ones that you will supply in future and redesign your workplace to suit

- Know your employees as individuals, not just someone who works for you. Get to know the life demands and diversity of each and make workplace adjustments to suit

Knowledge of your competitors is also essential – not just their products and services, but their people environments too. Remember, in the market for people, the best employers always get the best talent. Are they doing something that you are not?

Be keen to understand what motivates employees to stay with an employer - it is often not pay! In fact, most studies show that pay is 4th on the list; employees are always more keen on worklife balance and flexibility. In one study across all sectors, we measured that flexibility was first, followed by good leadership, personal development and then pay.

Is for Leadership, Learning and Lesson

In our family of origin, we learned to mimic the behaviour of our parents and guardians. So too do we look for example from our leaders. If sustained change is required, then leadership must behave in ways that create the desired culture. If they are inflexible, controlling and autocratic, then they will create a culture that behaves in a fearful, protective and closed way. Role modelling the culture you want is an important part of change. In essence, worklife balance should be led from the top.

Review your current leadership practices; do they work long hours, take work home and never share personal information? If so, then employees will do the same.

Work with your senior team to develop a clear and compelling vision of the where you want to get to. Communicate your vision, involve people in its development, articulation and realisation. Be consistent and celebrate success on the way. Use new leadership traits to ensure success. The key behaviours of future leaders are:

- Authenticity

- Recognising potential in others

- Empowering others through personal passion and risk taking

- Motivating others to seek opportunities and take risk

- Removing obstacles that prevent success

- Encouraging continuous improvement

- Celebrating success and learning from mistakes and failures

Being a good leader is meaningless if there is no one travelling with you...

"A leader 'all alone' is like the sound of one hand clapping" Joseph O'Connor.

Learning on the way doesn't just include formal training and coaching, it also means learning like a child does; trying things, failing, succeeding, playing, exploring and being curious. Maintain a child-like state and learn from every experience!

The lesson will come either in the moment or in the future as you reflect on where you have come from. Keep an open mind; the learning is in the wobbling! That means that just as toddlers wobble and fall down as they learn to walk, they never give in; they keep on wobbling until they master the art of walking... only then can they learn to run, jump, skip and dance.

Is for Motivation, Mother and Me-time

Motivation is made up of one part desire and one part expectation; both of which can be achieved through clear vision, good leadership and ownership for action. Motivating your team means understanding their personal strengths and releasing that potential. When people play to their strengths, they enjoy what they do and they do it well. They motivate each other and they strive for excellence. De-motivation comes from control, lack of choice and stifling talent. Create motivation through business and person-centred worklife balance strategies.

Seventy percent of women work outside the home and mothers account for a high percentage of the workforce; 1 in 6 has children under the age of 16. Little children are our future and finding ways to support family values and a mother's desire to work, means that as employers we must offer flexibility. Children cannot drive themselves to school or nursery and so rigid 9 to 5 working patterns exclude talent from applying for certain jobs. How can you rearrange work to suit different needs and still meet customer demand? As children grow, parents may request a different type of flexible working. For example, one employee who had worked part week whilst her children attended nursery, moved to term-time working when they went to school. 75% of professional women who are mothers also have a partner in full time employment. However, 74% of men in senior roles have a wife who stays at home. It is no wonder that women feel as though they have to work hard to gain recognition for their efforts and talent.

Me-time is time when you can just 'be'. It is time when you do not have to 'do' anything; time when you are a human being rather than a human doing. Calculate how many hours a week you have time to yourself; time to kick the leaves, listen to music, soak in a bath or just meditate. Schedule time in your diary each day; even if it is only half an hour to yourself. Taking a break from your work and life demands, allows you the space to think, plan and consider your life as a whole.

Is there a me-time activity that you have always wanted to do? Singing lessons? Piano lessons, Yoga, oil painting? If so, book your first session this week!

Is there a me-time activity that you could implement in the workplace? A library area? A sensory garden? A meditation room, a quiet room, or a prayer room? Think! Trial! Rollout!

Is for New, 'No!' and Need

New ways of working are sometimes a challenge to get used to, but the good news is that hundreds of organisations have already experimented and you can learn from them. Listen to their approaches and adapt best practice to suit your organisation. You can also download a copy of the flexible working matrix from our website, which provides information on what to consider for each of the popular flexible working practices. New cultures aren't developed overnight and may take up to 3 years to fully transition to a new state, so don't expect instant results. Take time to develop a strategy that will support a 3-year change programme and you will be able to implement new approaches over time.

Learning to say 'no!' to extra workload is difficult, however, it is important that organisations become wise to understand that whilst focusing on new business, they must also strip out waste and old legacy processes. Many organisations have downsized people, but forgot to downsize processes too, resulting in increased workload and stress. Saying 'no' to flexible working can also be challenging. However, in certain circumstances, it is legal to do so. It is essential to explore the options, review the business case and if there is a legitimate reason why you cannot allow the employee to work flexibly, then you will be able to refuse. However, do take legal advice. If you get it wrong, it could result in a claim against you. Try always to consider a compromise that may work for the business and the employee.

People need flexible working for 'reasons and seasons'. Reasons tend to be short term and often don't affect terms of employment. For example, flexing hours over the next two weeks to fit in study time for an impending exam. Seasons are generally longer term and for specific periods in someone's life. For example, an employee might be an athlete for their national team and during this phase of their life want to work a reduced working day so they can meet their sporting commitments. Requirements differ and it is essential that working patterns be flexible to suit short and long-term commitments. Business 'reasons and seasons' exist too and can include annualised hours for market seasonality and V-Time hours to manage supply and demand. For example, one organisation sells mainly to the tourist trade and although their shop was open 7 days a week, 364 days a year, it did very little trade during January and February. They moved to annualised hours and closed the shop during those months.

Is for Opportunity, Ownership and One

Opportunities rarely come labelled, but creating worklife balance is an opportunity that supports the business, the employee, the shareholder and ultimately the customer. Opportunities are there to be grabbed, but start small, offer new ways of working, deliver training to managers and then take the opportunity to measure and track the results. Worklife balance doesn't cost money, it saves money.

Ownership for worklife balance must be a partnership between the organisation and employee. That is because worklife balance is not just about policies and systems, but about people, their lives and their emotional commitments.

To really accelerate your worklife balance strategy, why not create key projects that can be owned by teams and other interested parties? For example, give ownership of projects like flexible working, women's networks, diversity, etc, to other teams. See 'Letter X' for more ideas.

What ONE thing can you do today to support people to achieve more balance in their life?

What ONE thing can you do to support your own worklife balance?

Who in your organisation could own ONE worklife initiative?

ONE also means 'one thing at a time' - success breeds success! When deciding who should own worklife balance, try always to identify:

1. A Champion - a senior manager who is an ally and someone who can organise spend

2. A Communicator - someone who loves to communicate, market and shout from the rooftops; someone who will be prepared to share best practice and support external communication too

3. A Visionary - someone who can create the future history, paint the picture of the success, create desire for change

4. A Planner - someone who can coordinate activities, track, measure and prioritise action

5. A Do-er - someone who is willing to pull a team together, roll their sleeves up and try things out. These people will pilot the ideas, be willing to make decisions and take a few risks

6. An Expert - Maybe someone from HR or an employment lawyer who can support the team with any legal aspects or policy decisions

7. An Evaluator - Someone who can track progress, review projects, keep things on track and report results

8. A Celebrator - someone who will mark major milestones and celebrate success.

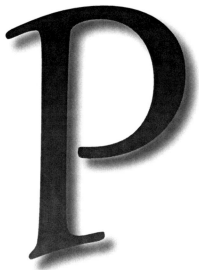

Is for Policy, Pilot and Presenteeism

Policy doesn't come first. Policy comes once you have established what works and what doesn't. Policy is the result of action not the catalyst for it. Experience shows that 'Policy first' results in; little take up, little empowerment, little confidence and little buy-in. After all, would you teach someone to drive by handing them a manual? Policies are useful for addressing legislative demands, defining approaches and procedures, but they do not change cultures by themselves. Policies that have to be in place for legal purposes are certainly necessary, however, do not be imprisoned by them! If it makes sense for your organisation to provide more benefits than the statutory minimum, then do so. For example, many organisations have variations on maternity leave, or sabbaticals. Where policies are in place, review them on a regular basis and involve staff in their development. For example, involve employees in policies like retirement, or holidays, or shift design.

Prior to policy try 'pilot'; pilot a new way of working in a department or team before writing the policy and rolling it out to all employees. Pilot studies are great ways to test the water to see if a new way of working will actually benefit the employee, the business or the customer. Once you have the evidence, then you can be sure that it may work elsewhere too. For example, an employee may wish to start work at 9:30 instead of 9:00, by piloting the new approach for 3-6 months, you can establish the impact on the team and the customer.

Presenteeism is based in FEAR. The manager that practices presenteeism believes that if the jacket is not on the back of the chair, then the employee cannot be working. FEAR stands for False Expectation Appearing Real - it is the manager's imagination that creates his fear. Working from home is a big 'no' for the presenteeism manager, as he believes that staff cannot be trusted to work whilst out of the office or out of his sight. Presenteeism does not guarantee productivity though and even if someone is at their desk it does not mean they are effective or efficient. Workload and interruptions usually mean that they are up to 27% less productive than their home-based colleague. Presenteeism is old style management practice and should be eradicated. Training your managers for consistency in implementation and to understand the business case is essential to success.

Presenteeism also leads to a long-hours culture, as employees begin to believe that being present is an indicator of loyalty, commitment, route to promotion and recognition of hard work.

For some, working long hours is personal choice, and that is fine, personal choice is to be encouraged; as long as it is not having a detrimental affect on their, or other people's, health & safety. However, those that feel they have no choice but to work long hours, feel a real sense of imbalance; a tug of war between life and work demands.

Worklife balance is achieved when the employee feels as though they have CHOICE; choice to work long hours when the workload demands it, and choice to take time back for life when it doesn't. A manager's job is to ensure that long hours doesn't become the way of life for all employees.

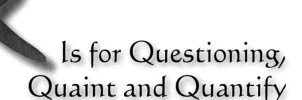

Is for Questioning, Quaint and Quantify

Question the status quo. Ask, "Why do we do it this way? Is there a legitimate business reason or is it a custom that could be challenged?" or "What do our internal and external customers want from us and are we there when they really need us?" or "Is there a better way to deliver our product or service that would help employees to balance their lives whilst still delivering excellent service to our customers?"

Encourage employees to question the status quo too by developing a process improvement mentality. For example, one organisation has a system called "Dare to Do it Differently" where challenge, risk and questioning are core to improvements made. Set up an employee suggestion scheme or a process improvement scheme. Up to 75% of a process can be stripped out because it is not directly focused on the customer. By stripping out waste and unnecessary workload, you free up time for more balance.

Many of the processes that we hold onto are quaint legacies that do not serve today's workplace. If you have been in an organisation for many years, you may not recognise these quaint little traditions because you are so used to them! One company who staged a 'bring your kids to work day' stripped out 22 quaint processes because their children asked 'why do you do that?' Out of the mouth of babes! But sometimes a fresh pair of eyes helps us to see what we have become accustomed to. Job swaps and job rotations are internal ways to identify quaint and legacy processes.

You cannot know how much you have improved unless you quantify it. With process improvement, the key measures are time and accuracy. By improving both of these, you improve productivity and business results. Dr. Edwards Deming said that 95% of fault, when something goes wrong, is due to the process and not the person. Therefore instead of cultivating a culture of blame, develop a culture of improvement. Workload improvement and process improvement can only be trained in an experiential way. The most inspiring and globally successful training is called 6 Step Improvement; details are contained at the end of this book. Quantify the gains you make and use those measures to set goals for improvement.

Benchmarking best practice from other organisations is a good way to accelerate your change programme. You can do this through a Benchmark Study Visit organised by The Worklife Company or access some of the Case Studies on our website as a first step.

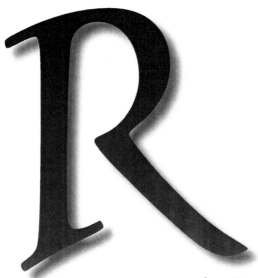

Is for Responsibility, Reasons and Recognition

Responsibilities outside of work will always take priority. If employees are given responsibility, they act responsibly. In response, many organisations now offer 'Responsibility Leave' to all employees. This is paid leave that can be taken in hour long blocks of time. Usually, it is between 24 and 40 hours per year (3 to 5 days). An employee can take the hours to cover life responsibilitues (sports days, dentist appointments etc) or emergencies (broken car, sick child, flood etc). It is normally under-used as employees do not take advantage of the benefit or the trust. Good organisations respond to this by linking unused Responsibility Leave to recognition and allow employees to take up to 2 days of it as 'me-time', Christmas shopping time or Birthday time. One company implemented 24 hours (3 days) of Responsibility Leave for people to take when needed. The employer found that instead of taking a whole day off, employees took a couple of hours, or half a day to deal with the emergency or life commitment. Sickness absence reduced by 84% and productivity increased by 37%.

People do not come to work to take advantage; some will, but are a minority and it is your responsibility to manage their poor performance in a timely and appropriate fashion. However, most don't and it is not appropriate to treat the other 95% of employees in a distrustful way! If an employee, who is normally a good performer, has a reason to be at home because of a life issue, then help them by allowing them to do so through Responsibility Leave or flexible working; like working from home. If their job is office based, what tasks of yours can you delegate to them to do at home? If their job is office based and you cannot give them work, allow the time out and agree a plan to either make up the hours when they return, take holiday, unpaid leave, Responsibility Leave or waive the lost hours (especially if they are good performers). The reasons people need time out are many and varied. Your job is to reduce the stress of worrying about work, when they are already worried about life.

Recognition works best when it is regarded as such by the receiver. Therefore get to know your people and what they regard as recognition. Time is often better than money as it is less likely to encourage an 'entitlement' culture. Remember, what is reward to one can be punishment to another. Days off for Birthdays are good recognition tools and something you can give to everyone!

Is for Self, Strengths and Stress

On the scales of worklife, time for self is often forgotten. When was the last time that you took time out just for you, to do something that you enjoy, or do something that would improve your personal development? Book me-time into your diary as you would any other scheduled event. The difference is that this is time just for you; and be sure not to let anyone tell you how to spend it! For many, it is pamper time, or a walk in the park, spiritual time, or a snooze under the duvet! It can even be thinking time at work when you are not attending meetings, doing email or writing reports! Getting time to innovate, come up with new ideas and strategies are often regarded as a luxury, but it is essential, so book a meeting with yourself. Go for a walk round the car park, or if you work in a city, find a quiet space (out of the office) to contemplate. Many organisations are setting up quiet space in the office for people to just think. These are one-person meeting points and quiet booths.

Many organisations are moving towards a strengths based approach to employment of people. That means looking at each individual and identifying their unique strengths and linking that with their role. So instead of spending and wasting phenomenal amounts of money trying to improve weaknesses, these employers develop strengths. The result is more worklife balance; people who do what they love, love what they do, do it quicker, better and with more innovation. Continually focusing on people's weaknesses is demotivating, expensive and stressful; for the employer as well as the employee.

Stress is a major issue in business today and the main causes are workload, lack of balance, performance cultures and a negative culture. Manage stress effectively by identifying and eliminating the root cause. Provide access to stress management techniques, like wellbeing initiatives, relaxation, counselling, coaching and creative workshops that encourage self awareness, creativity and self exploration. In the workplace, explore the environment, the leadership style, the diversity of people, the physical environment and of course working practices to look for ways to reduce stress. Release the potential of your business and your people by focusing on potential not weaknesses to relieve stress and absence. Providing good nutrition, regular breaks and workplace exercise classes also helps. Work+ measures the physical and emotional environment, see the back of the book for details.

Is for Time, Talent and Transition

Time waits for no man, time is money, time is running away! All of these folk sayings imply that time is short and should be used wisely. As an organisation, how often do you stand back and look at how you spend time? What activities add value to the customer and what are just old legacies? Carrying out a review of how you spend time highlights areas for improvement. If the focus is on saving time at work and adding it to life, a team away day, or a team social event once in a while, then this will motivate the team to create change. People are busy, but are they focused on doing the right things? Workload has a habit of building up and often nothing drops off the list. Long hours result and often for managers, that means staying late to catch up on all the things that didn't get done in the day. Long hours at middle management level are often an indicator of this.

Managing talent includes the provision of time for employees to innovate. One client insists on 20% of time being focused on developing new ideas. The afternoon is often a better time for creativity, therefore schedule creative brainstorming sessions in the afternoon when everyone is physically more able to be creative.

Transition towards a culture of worklife balance sometimes means having to deal with negative as well as positive emotions. For example, negative emotion can include backlash from managers who need to let go of the control they have always had. It can also include backlash from certain employees who feel they do not have the flexibility that others enjoy. Managing emotional turmoil during transition is essential to the success of your worklife balance strategy. Networks, sharing best practice, internal briefings, and a continuous focus on what is right for the business can help people move through this change.

Make sure that you engage a team whose responsibility is to manage the transition phase. They should creatively communicate progress, initiatives, results, best practices, training and development and most of all they should engage in dialogue. Setting up networks, like a women's network, a wellbeing network, a faith-friendly network, a gay and lesbian network or a graduate network all help to create open dialogue and prevent backlash. One client has set up a worklife balance communication suite with social networks on their intranet site, a chat room and a physical cafe dedicated to network meetings.

Is for Universal, Understanding and Unleash

Creating worklife balance is a business decision and should be part of the business strategy. This is not something that can be delegated to HR. HR's job is to support by providing strategic consulting, infrastructure design, training, legal advice and policy etc. A universal approach to worklife balance that includes all people strategy as part of the business strategy, and owned by the senior team, provides the best results. This then becomes the way that you manage your people, not an extra thing to do. Begin by asking "Where do we want this business to be in 5 years time?" See it in terms of vision, not numbers! Then ask "What kind of people do we need to get us there?" Use scenario planning and HR strategy tools to build your people strategy linked to your vision.

Take time to gain a real understanding of flexible working options and how they will support your business and its customers. We have 1440 minutes in a day, 7 days in a week, 52 weeks in a year and 10 years in a decade. Why then do we always focus on the 'working day' and how many hours people spend at work? In one client I know of, 2 finance directors who job share a year cut the hours and weeks to suit the tasks they are employed to do. I know of another who works hours as part of a consultancy; they close in July and August, their quietest months. Another employs people based on their body clocks and rhythms – larks and owls! It is fine to rip up the rule books on time and look at what will make a real difference to your productivity and business results. Control people by the clock and you trap potential.

Unleash the creativity in your business, look for ways to build idea workshops, engage people to ghost others to look for new and better ways to do things. Release talent by encouraging the dreamers; take your dreams to the community. One team of senior managers was forced to have a 3 month sabbatical from the business to support a local community project to build a sensory garden for the blind. After 3 months, they came back to their own business with renewed vigour and creativity, but also with their own eyes finally able to see what improvements they had been blind to in their own organisation. Your people are your business, not just your financial results.

Is for Virtual, Visionary and Victory

Managing a virtual team is becoming more common, especially in sectors where real estate is expensive and usage is low. As more employees begin to work from home, work different shifts and work in different locations from their manager, it becomes more necessary to have different practices and systems in place to manage your virtual organisation. For example, performance management systems that depend more on 360 degree feedback from customers, employees peers and suppliers to ensure a fair measure of the remote worker's contribution.

The employee also needs to feel part of a team and so effective communication is essential. It is not enough to hold weekly teleconferences! Managers should include regular face-to-face time. When meeting as a team, it should include team-building activities as well as task reviews, otherwise people will feel as though they are only regarded for what they do, rather than who they are. It is also essential to be able to manage the physical and emotional environment for the remote worker. For example, if your team is home-based and you have an employee with a very young family, it may be difficult for them to concentrate whilst at home. Therefore, split site working may be of benefit to these employees.

Visionary leaders can express their image of the future workplace. Many predict more virtual environments, foggier hierarchies and fluid portfolio careers. This may be true for some, but what will it be like for your team and organisation? Conducting a future-world exercise with your team will support you to consider tomorrow's physical, emotional and business environment. Download the Paper Coach for this exercise from the website.

Victory is achievement of a goal. Before you begin, and as part of your plan, decide how you will celebrate the small wins as well as the big. It doesn't need to be all bells and whistles; just a thank you card to those involved will be celebration enough for certain milestones. When working with one CEO to improve his time management, I noticed that two days per month were blocked out in his diary. I asked him what these days were set aside for. He told me "Leave those days! They're not to be touched! They are the two most important days in my calendar." I asked why, and he replied "I have 600 people who work for me, and every month when it is pay day, I personally walk round the shop floor, I shake each person's hand, I hand them their pay cheque and I thank them for the work and effort that they have made during the month. It takes me two full days to see everyone and it is time well spent. I learn so much from those men and women as I stop to chat, listen to their ideas, their needs and their moans too! Without those 600 hard-working and dedicated people, I would not have this job or this company. It's the least I can do to give them my dedicated time just once a month.

Is for Wellbeing, Women and Workload

Managing the wellbeing of employees is a positive and active initiative that any size of company can engage in. Programmes vary and often include initiatives like:

- Physical wellbeing: exercise, nutrition, massage, aromatherapy, homeopathy, health checks, medical checks etc.

- Mental wellbeing: stress management, wellbeing audits, stress surveys, coaching, counselling, meditation, alternative therapies

Corporate Social Responsibility projects can often be linked to wellbeing too, for example, 10k walks for charitable organisations which combine physical wellbeing with charitable giving. Alternatively, trivia quizzes boost teamwork and maybe even mental agility, whilst also giving to a nominated charity. Even if you are a micro business, you can still involve employees in wellbeing activities. For example, a small Nursery organises lunchtime walks for staff to encourage exercise and a break from the Setting. They encourage healthy eating for the staff and children too, resulting in 100% attendance.

Women account for just over 50% of the population and yet are not equally represented in management. There are many reasons for this and the solution is complex. However, from a worklife balance perspective: 85% of the caring responsibilities in a family remain with women, 1 in 6 women in the workplace has children under the age of 16. 49% of women with caring responsibilities need to work reduced hours and many companies still insist on management roles being full time and often extended time with high levels of travel or overnight stays. Flexibility is key to women at all levels and yet, in the 10 years after having a child, only 4% of women are ever promoted. Flexible working for all would provide a timely and simple solution that would benefit everyone and allow for more diversity in leadership.

Workload is increasing and performance cultures continue to insist on 'more for less'. Sadly, the message to employees is 'work harder' and 'cut costs', but working harder doesn't necessarily mean working smarter, because working harder often equates to working longer. We need to become smarter about who does what and when they do it. Workload overload is the biggest enemy to balance; therefore it needs to be managed effectively through performance management linked to a balanced scorecard, business plan and a culture change programme.

Is for eXciting, X-Shaped and Xenophobic

Worklife balance can be fearful for many organisations. They believe that it will cost money, time and the biggest fear of all, is that it will open the floodgates to all employees requesting flexible working. However, quick wins, pilot studies and successes prove all fears to be unfounded (remember, FEAR stands for False Expectation Appearing Real). These fears and worries paralyse organisations and prevent them from moving forward. They limit organisational success and people potential. Try something new that creates excitement, empowerment and willingness to change. Excitement is the fuel of change and comes as a result of releasing creative potential and passion for a positive future.

Many organisations understand 'what' worklife balance is, but struggle with 'how' to implement it. X-shaped worklife balance provides a framework for the 'how'. The point at the four corners of the letter X represent a different aspect of worklife balance, more details can be downloaded from our website and refer to page V at the start of the book. The four initiatives are:

1. Leadership commitment and involvement
2. Training, education and communication
3. Flexible working and other work practices
4. Measures, tracking and change

By linking all of these, the champions of culture change can provide clear guidance on how to implement a forward thinking worklife balance culture and report on how well each initiative is progressing. That is because they sit at the centre of the X, with a clear view of the four corners.

Xenophobia can and does exist in organisations. It means prejudice, or at an unconscious level can include misinterpretation or simply having the wrong impression. In worklife balance terms, this can be dangerous as it creates assumptions "she's a mum, therefore she will want part time!" or "He's young and single, he won't mind working longer hours." Stereotyping groups creates prejudice and this can stifle a worklife balance project. It is essential to explore all systems, like recruitment, promotion and flexible working to ensure that xenophobic behaviours do not exist - either overtly or covertly in the system itself! During worklife balance training and coaching, ensure that the emotional aspects of flexible working are explored to prevent Xenophobia.

Is for 'Yes!', Young and Year

Say YES to worklife balance, as it makes clear business sense. If you don't, your competitors will and employees will be quick to go where they will be supported. The culture you have is therefore a recruitment and retention decision – are you attracting or retaining the best?

Say YES to worklife balance as it makes customer sense. Customers will be loyal to those organisations that can give them what they want, when they want it. They also wish to deal with bright-eyed and bushy-tailed employees, not long-hours zombies. Doing business with your people should be a pleasure.

Say YES to worklife balance as it makes people sense. Employees that are trusted are more motivated and committed. They are happy in work and take that positive regard back to their families and communities, thereby creating values and social structures that civilised nations thrive on.

The young want flexibility from the start of their employment and will join an employer if it can provide the right environment for them. Flexibility of time and place means that the young employees regard time and work differently. Download the research from our website, to understand more about the young worker.

Your needs for worklife balance will change. What will suit you now, may not suit you next week, next year or in ten years time. Take time to measure your worklife balance right now. Consider carrying out a worklife survey, stress audit or focus groups to establish causes of imbalance or needs. Once you know what you need, you can create new approaches to working. Pilot new practices quickly in order to gain momentum, and always track results.

Do not be imprisoned by yesterday's methods. What worked yesterday, may not work for your business tomorrow. Living your business life 'walking backwards' will prevent you from seeing opportunities for tomorrow. Yesterday is in the past; let it go once you have learned the lessons of improvement for the future. Look at a 'year in the life of worklife balance' as a way of communicating what you have achieved and also what you will achieve during the forthcoming year. A year of events, calendars and initiatives is a good way to engage people and define what will be done during the year. It also helps you to focus the long term plan into year-long budgeted initiatives. One organisation has one big initiative for each of the four X-shaped initiatives. That allows them to focus on what they will do each year to suit their organisation and its people.

Is for Zeal, Zest and Zenith...and Zzzz!

Zeal is energy and after about 18 months into a worklife balance project, all of a sudden there is a ground swell of energy that really takes hold. Leaders, managers and employees suddenly realise the business benefits of worklife balance and there is a sudden zeal or determination to do more. By this time, the basics are in place and people are keen to look outside to learn from others. This is where the zest for benchmarking is born and the need to compare using external measures. There are many external accreditation systems that will help and support your organisation to measure and compare yourself to others. There are 'Best Business' awards too, which if taken seriously, provide the zest and zeal to be the best.

For example, a department within a large firm of lawyers decided to apply for an external award. They worked hard to put together their application. They were chosen as finalists by the judging panel, were invited to the very prestigious awards' dinner and were thrilled and delighted to be awarded the top prize. The thrill of winning was soon shared across the organisation providing more commitment and zeal to further improve their working environment. It is always a good idea to communicate best practice in a way that is full of zest too. The purpose of communication is to change behaviour, so be creative in the way that you do this. For example, one client, who makes sandwiches for local supermarkets decided to use one of their triangular packages to communicate their vision and strategy for worklife balance. The front of the packaging announced the vision and content of the strategy, the 'ingredients' label announced more additives, like flexible working, more teamwork, etc. On the 'Nutritional Value' label, it mentioned more motivation, better wellbeing etc. Be creative. Communicate in a way that engages your team.

When you reach your Zenith, it means that you have reached the goal of becoming an employer of choice. At this stage, you can look back down the valley from where you have travelled. You can acknowledge the path that you have taken, and from this vantage point and with hindsight, you may even observe shortcuts or wished you'd done things differently. You notice the good times, the challenges and the triumphs. Be proud., You have reached the top; one of the best companies to work for and stay with. Well done!

Finally, sleep eazzzy, knowing that worklife balance creates buzz and makes buzziness sense. Zzzzzz...

A to Z Summary

Worklife Balance

- Is an investment in your future
- Atracts and retains talent
- Creates flexibility and choice
- Creates inclusion - fairness to all
- Releases potential of people and business
- Ensures bottom line benefits
- Attracts and retains customers

Priorities for action are:

- Gain leadership support, commitment and involvement
- Keep it focused on the business as well as the individual
- Training, coaching, mentoring and share-fairs for consistency - especially management development
- Create involvement - listen to the diversity of your teams and business
- Change the people measures - contribution, not hours!
- Measure the business results
- Develop policies that communicate the behaviours and culture you want
- Develop a communication strategy that works
- Benchmark with the best and share best practice

Popular and common flexible working options.

Reduced Hours

- Part time
- Job share
- Annualised hours
- Term time working
- Zero hours contracts
- V-time working
- Interim working
- Flex force working (peak times)
- Sabbaticals
- Career breaks
- Phased return and leave (usually linked to maternity, leave of absence, illness and retirement)

Re-Arranged Hours

- Compressed working year/month/fortnight/ week
- Flexi-time
- Staggered hours
- Shift working
- Self rostering
- Teleworking
- Flexi-place
- Working from home/ Home-based working
- Ergo-hours
- Career breaks
- Time Sovereignty

Message from the Author

"May I wish you well on your journey to becoming a great place to work. After all, work takes up over a third of our lives, and therefore it should be a great place to be; not a Monday through Friday sort of dying.

However, every journey must begin with an understanding of where you are today and where you are going. That means reviewing current practices, measuring and diagnosing organisational culture, leadership and infrastructure. It also means reviewing management consistency and measuring employee satisfaction. Only then can you build a clear vision of 'what' employer of choice means to you and your people.

More and more I am asked to deliver keynote presentations to inspire change in organisations, but I always say, even though I may inspire, it is the implementation of what I say that is key and yet difficult for some. Therefore, I have produced some additional resources, measurement tools, workshops and diagnostics that will help you to take, and stay on, the right path. If you want to get things moving in your organisation and you are struggling to convince the Board, or you have a worklife balance programme that deserves a mid-life kick, then call; I may provide an inspiring catalyst for change."

Lynne Copp

Author

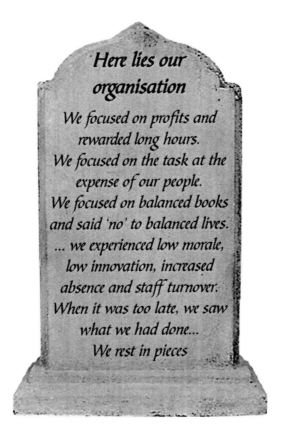

Here lies our organisation
We focused on profits and rewarded long hours.
We focused on the task at the expense of our people.
We focused on balanced books and said 'no' to balanced lives.
... we experienced low morale, low innovation, increased absence and staff turnover.
When it was too late, we saw what we had done...
We rest in pieces

Remember...

No one EVER lay on their deathbed wishing they'd spent more time at work!

Contact the Author

Lynne Copp
Managing Director

The Worklife Company
The Lindens,
High Street,
Burbage,
Marlborough,
Wiltshire,
SN8 3AF
UK

t: +44 (0)1672 811170

e: info@theworklifecompany.com
i: www.theworklifecompany.com

Other books in this series which will be in print soon:

Life is a Ship - The A to Z of Worklife Balance for Individuals
The A to Z of Worklife Balance for Women

Other books by the Author which will be in print soon:

Dancing 'Round the Handbags
The Emperor's New Business Clothes

To order copies of these books or for more information please go to www.lollypoppublishing.co.uk

Further Information available includes

SkillSnax® - 90 minute bite-sized learning. Everything from Managing Worklife Balance to Managing Workload and Nutrition for the Brain at Work.

Dancing Round the Handbags® - book and workshop aimed entirely at professional women to support them to stop juggling and start balancing work and life.

Worklife Evolution® - diagnostic tool to measure maturity in worklife balance and provide recommendations for future strategy.

Timeout - 2 day programme aimed at managers and leaders to support them with vision, worklife balance and personal wellbeing.

Worklife Coaching - Coaching for managers to support worklife balance, individual coaching to achieve worklife balance and wellbeing.

Coach the Coach programmes to train internal coaches to coach worklife balance.

Stop Juggling & Start Balancing Work & Life - a programme aimed at employees to support them to take stock of their work and life and build personal and career strategies to improve both.

CHOICES - Career and life development programme which focuses on long term goals for work and life. Highly creative and innovative programme which includes bite-sized coaching sessions.

Bump to Babe to Business® - Support and coaching services for women during pregnancy, childcare choices and back to work.

Six Step Improvement - A simulation training programme to support leaders, managers and employees to identify workload issues and methods for process improvement. Can be built with additional flexible modules.

For more resources please contact the Author Lynne Copp

Thank you

Lightning Source UK Ltd.
Milton Keynes UK
14 October 2009

144967UK00002B/108/P